SRA
OPEN COURT
READING

Tom and Pop

SRA

A Division of The McGraw·Hill Companies

Columbus, Ohio

www.sra4kids.com

SRA/McGraw-Hill

A Division of The **McGraw·Hill** Companies

Copyright © 2002 by SRA/McGraw-Hill.

Printed in the United States of America.

Send all inquiries to:
SRA/McGraw-Hill
8787 Orion Place
Columbus, OH 43240-4027

ISBN 0-07-569430-1
   3 4 5 6 7 8 9 DBH 05 04 03 02

Tom is hot.

Tom hops in the pond.

The pond is not hot.

Tom's pop has a pot.

The pot is on top.
The pot is on Pop.

Tom and Pop are not hot.